Pitching with the Papelbons

"We would like to thank you very much for taking the time to read this book. We all love playing baseball and hope that this book will help teach you many of the things we have learned to achieve success in baseball. We believe it's important to always practice hard, be a good teammate and listen to your coach. If you do all of those things then you are well on your way to having a fun and successful baseball career." - **Jonathan, Jeremy, & Joshua Papelbon.**

Written By Jon and Lauren Goode

Illustrated by Rachel Gregorio

It's Saturday morning and big brother Jonathan, along with younger brother twins Jeremy and Joshua, sit down for breakfast before the baseball game. "Are you boys ready for the big game today?" asks Mom. "I was born ready and I'm ready to win," says big brother Jonathan. "Now just remember it's not about winning or losing, but it's about trying your best all the time. Okay?" said Dad, who is also the coach of the team. "Okay," the boys answer together, but laughing because they know they really want to win.

The weather is perfect. It's sunny and warm and Jonathan is ready to start the game. He quickly strikes out the first three batters. This is the perfect start to the game and reminds Jonathan why practicing and listening to his coaches is important. "I love baseball," Jonathan thinks to himself.

In the top of the third inning, Jonathan, Jeremy, and Joshua have a reason to cheer. Their teammate Kylan hits a home run scoring Brayden and Kenzley giving them a 3-0 lead!

In the bottom of the third inning, Jonathan gets two outs quickly, but gives up a double. With the other team having a chance to score, Coach Papelbon decides to send in a relief pitcher, Jeremy.

Jonathan did a great job, but now it's up to Jeremy!

With the runner on second, Jeremy gets ready to pitch. The batter is surprised because this Papelbon pitcher is not throwing with his right hand. He is throwing with his left hand!

With three pitches, Jeremy strikes out the batter, keeping the lead 3-0.

"I knew I could do it," Jeremy thinks to himself.

The game now heads to the final inning. Needing only three more outs to win the game, Coach Papelbon turns to Joshua to save the game.

If Joshua can get these three outs, the entire Papelbon family will have pitched a shutout. Joshua begins to warm up and the other team is even more confused because this Papelbon is throwing submarine!

Joshua quickly gets two outs and one more will win the game! He gets two strikes on the batter and hears Jeremy and Jonathan shout from the dugout, "You can do it!"

Joshua winds up with the pitch and throws it as hard as he can. The batter swings and misses and they win 3-0!!

The two teams line up to shake hands because it's important to have good sportsmanship. Jonathan, Jeremy, and Joshua are so proud of themselves for pitching a shutout together and winning the game.

"You boys did a great job, but remember, it's not about winning or losing but trying your best, and you boys did that," said Mom. "You're right Mom," the boys answered together, but once again they laughed because they won, which is what they wanted from the start.

We would like to thank the Papelbon family for allowing us to write this book and allowing us to use the pictures of Jonathan, Jeremy and Joshua as kids. In particular a special thank you to Sheila Papelbon for all her help with this book.
- **Jon and Lauren Goode**

The C² Mission is a charitable 501C-3 foundation to benefit children and families affected by Cerebral Palsy (CP) and Cystic Fibrosis (CF) in the New England area.

The goals of the C² Mission are to provide financial support for families in the New England area affected by CF and CP, assisting area CF and CP charities with existing fundraisers, and most importantly providing hope and smiles to anyone affected by CF and CP. The C² Mission is "a Mission of Hope."

For more information on the C² Mission please visit the website at c2mission.org.

ISBN: 978-1-60461-804-4